Raimo Suikkari

Helsinki

Sights and Attractions

Photo sources:
Sakari Viika, page 55
Lentokuva Vallas,
pages 4, 7 (top), 10-11,
36-37 and 67 (bottom)

Data sources:
Helsinki City Tourist Office
Moorhouse-Michael Carapetian –
Leena Ahtola-Moorhouse:
Helsingin jugendarkkitehtuuri
Anne Borg: Senaatintori
Nils Erik Wikberg: Senaatintori

Original text, photographs and implementation:
Raimo Suikkari/RKS Tietopalvelu Oy
Publisher: RKS Tietopalvelu Oy
Layout: Hanna-Mari Ruohonen
Translation: Marianne Lindahl
Colour separation: Scan World Oy, Helsinki
Printed by Gummerus Printing, Jyväskylä 2004
3rd edition
Hardback ISBN 952-5308-13-8
Paperback ISBN 952-5308-12-X

Raimo Suikkari

Helsinki

Sights and Attractions

Helsinki —
"Daughter of the Baltic"

The predominant element of Helsinki is the sea. In summer, its harbours are adorned by thousands of boats, from small sailboats to huge luxury cruisers. As much as 501 km^2 of the city´s total area of 686 km^2 is water. The Helsinki archipelago has many interesting sights, like the Suomenlinna fortress island and the Korkeasaari Zoo. These can be reached by ferry or sightseeing boat from the Market Square.

Helsinki is a mecca for the tourist looking for exceptional events, such as the many cultural and sports happenings in Kaivopuisto, a beautiful park in the elegant residential southern part of the city. But even a quiet stroll on the snow-covered ice can be an unforgettable experience. A trip to be remembered is a cruise on board the s/s Helena or the m/s Runeberg.

The local tourist offices offer all kinds of guided boat tours. On many of them a delicious meal is served on board. Helsinki is a lively and dynamic little metropolis, but nature is within easy reach from the city centre.

A trip on board one of the sightseeing boats leaving from the Market square gives a good overall view of the shores and islands of Helsinki and its archipelago. Besides admiring the lovely sights, the passengers can enjoy a snack or a delicious meal on board.

5

The Suomenlinna fortress can be visited also in winter. Although the sea is covered with ice, the passage to the island is kept open. It is advisable to reserve a whole day for a visit to the museums, parks, restaurants and historical sights of this remarkable old fortress. Suomenlinna was declared a World Heritage Site by Unesco in 1991. The trip by boat takes only 15 minutes.

In summer, the harbours of Helsinki are visited by ships from all over the world. S/s Cuauhtemoc has come all the way from Mexico.

The Korkeasaari zoo can be reached by water bus from the Market Square or by bridge from Mustikkamaa. The zoo is open to the public during the whole year.

The Baltic Herring Market in Helsinki is a 250 year-old tradition. It takes place in the Market Square in October every year. At this week-long event you can find Baltic herring prepared in every imaginable way. The market also offers exciting events, like dancing to live music.

Ice-breakers keep the sea passages open in winter. In summer they are moored at the Katajanokka quay (right, top).

In winter, the temperature can fall below 20 degrees.
It is cold, but the morning sun shines through the icy mist.
Spring is on its way!

Tourists marvel at this typically Finnish phenomenon: rugs and carpets being washed in the sea in Kaivopuisto. (left)

Helsinki seen from the Market place harbour - a spectacular sight.

The Market Square — the Heart of Helsinki

To the tourist arriving by boat, the Market Square is within easy reach. Fruit, vegetables, fish, handicrafts and hand-made souvenirs are on sale at this lively outdoor market, bordered by the harbour and many historically interesting buildings. Here, the atmosphere is lively and spontaneous, and the customer is greeted with a friendly smile.

In summer, sightseeing boats and water buses leave from the Market Square for guided cruises to the Helsinki archipelago or to the Suomenlinna fortress island and the Korkeasaari zoo.

The Market Square is only a stone's throw away from the South harbour. (top)

The Empress' Stone (Keisarinnan kivi) in the centre of the Market Square is the oldest monument in Helsinki. This obelisk, designed by Carl Ludwig Engel, was unveiled in 1835 in remembrance of the first visit to Helsinki in 1833 by czar Nikolai I and czarina Alexandra. The monument is situated on the very spot where the royal guests got off their ship Izhora – the first steam ship ever to visit Helsinki.

The fountain statue Havis Amanda, a mermaid surrounded by sea-lions, was created by sculptor Ville Vallgren in 1908. The basin is designed by architect Eliel Saarinen. The statue is a cult destination for the May Day student festival, on which occasion the maiden is washed, dressed and adorned with a students' cap (left).

The oldest market hall in Helsinki is situated on the southwestern side of the Market Square. It was built in 1888 and designed by Gustaf Nyström. Here you can buy all kinds of delicacies; meat, fish, pastries, bread and cheese. There is also a café and a souvenir shop (bottom).

At the Market Square you can buy anything from food to hand-made dolls and jewellery and Christmas trees in winter.
The music, the seagulls and the lively commerce create a warm and friendly atmosphere.

The Senaatintori Square and the Neo-classical Centre

In the 17th century the site which is now known as the Senaatintori Square comprised a market place, a church and a graveyard. A great part of the city was destroyed during the Great Nordic War, and the reconstruction of the buildings surrounding the square was started in 1721. Today, the square is the scene for many cultural activities and all kinds of events. Here, Independence Day is celebrated each year on 6th December with sparkling fireworks.

The Senaatintori square is surrounded by monumental neo-classical buildings designed by Carl Ludwig Engel (1778-1840). On the western side of the square is the impressive main building of the Helsinki University, (completed in 1832) and the splendid University Library. On the eastern side is the Government Palace, which is the headquarters of the Government and the Prime Minister. In the so called Presidential Hall of this building, the laws of Finland are ratified by the President.

In the middle of the square is the statue of czar Alexander II, who was favourably inclined towards reforms and highly appreciated by the people of Finland. The statue was sculpted by Walter Runeberg in 1894. The figures below feature Jurisprudence (Lex), Peace (Pax), Light (Lux) and Work (Labour).

The beautiful Cathedral and its green central dome is a dominating element in the Senaatintori Square. This is another of Engel's projects, planned in 1830. After his death 10 years later, Ernst Lohrmann added four small towers around the central dome and two side pavilions. The work was completed in 1852. The Cathedral is the most popular of Helsinki's tourist attractions. The Senaatintori square is a forum for all kinds of events. From the steps of the Cathedral you have a magnificent view of the Market Square and the South harbour.

The place where the former Ulrika Eleonora Church was situated is marked in the pavement of Senaatintori Square. A magnificent snow church is being built here in winter (left).

Besides regular parish church services, services for Parliament and the University are held in the Cathedral.

The Government Palace, the University, the Cathedral and the buildings on the southern side of the Senaatintori Square form a rare example of neo-classical continuity. The main building of Helsinki University (bottom), on the western side of the Senaatintori Square was designed by Engel. Its façade decorations and proportions are similar to those of the Government Palace (top).

Interior view of the Helsinki University Library (left).

The"White Hall" (Valkoinen Sali) in Aleksanterinkatu 16-18 was built in 1925 and designed by Walter Jung. Today it is used for cultural events, exhibitions and seminars.
The brown red building to the left is the official residence of the Mayor of Helsinki (top).

The oldest stone house in the city of Helsinki is this building on the southeastern side of the Senaatintori square. It is called the Sederholm residence. It was built by merchant Johan Sederholm in 1757. (left, bottom)

The City Hall north of the Market Square is designed by German architect Carl Ludwig Engel.
It was originally built in 1883, but has later been rebuilt, except for the façade and the big auditorium. The reconstruction was designed by Aarno Ruusuvuori.

Architecture, City Sights and Attractions

The architecture of Helsinki offers a fascinating intersection of the city's colourful history, with influences from both East and West.

Nordic simplicity and refinement are reflected in many architectural styles, and the ever changing light gives the colours a different depth during each season. The beauty of the buildings is enhanced by the parks and the sea.

The best known architectural sight in Helsinki is the monumental neo-classical centre created by Johan Albrecht Ehrenström and Carl Ludwig Engel.

Helsinki can be experienced in many different ways. Walking is the best way of seeing the city, but you can also take a tour on one of the yellow/green city bicycles. Serial tickets, such as the very popular Helsinki Card, are available for buses, trams and the metro. The Helsinki Card also gives you free entrance to museums and exhibitions around the city. In summer, helpful and friendly Helsinki-guides in green uniforms are there to help visitors find their way, and the Tourist Information Office at Pohjoisesplanadi 19 is at your service with all the information you may need.

Pohjoisespladi is a popular shopping street with many cafés. The European Commission Representation in Finland and the Helsinki Travel Agency are located in this street.

The beautiful Esplanadi Park is Helsinki's favourite promenade and meeting place.
It was already included in the city plan made by J.A. Ehrenström in 1812.

Kaivopuisto is a fashionable residential area favoured by diplomats.
The Kaivopuisto park has comfortable lawns and paths, lively cafés and a small observatory.
The park is a popular place for outings and picnics .
On Labour Day on the 1st of May, students begin the celebration by gathering on the Observatory Hill
(Ullanlinna). (bottom)

In winter, the statues and parks
are covered with snow. The sun is
shining on the massive buildings
in Pohjoisesplanadi. The statue of
Finland´s national poet
J.L.Runeberg (1804-1877) was
sculpted by his son Walker
Runeberg in 1885 (bottom)

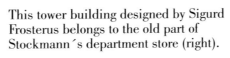

This tower building designed by Sigurd
Frosterus belongs to the old part of
Stockmann´s department store (right).

The villa quarters in Eira and Ullanlinna are some of the city's finest architectural sights.
The picture shows a villa in Eira, designed by Werner von Essen, and built in 1911.
To the left, a statue of famous Finnish author Juhani Aho (1861-1921), sculpted by Aimo Tukiainen in 1961
(top).

These individual art-nouveau houses in Huvilakatu makes you think of an idyllic small-town street.
The buildings form a beautiful, uniform continuity. The dwelling area is on two floors, and the roof
construction and the ground floor give additional space (right, top).

One of the oldest preserved wooden houses in Helsinki is the Burgher's House (Ruiskumestarin talo) in
Kristianinkatu 12 in the quarter of Kruunuhaka. It was built in 1832. Today it is open to the public as a part
of the Helsinki City Museum (right, bottom).

The German Church (Johanneksen kirkko), built in 1864, is a popular place for weddings (left).

The Uspenski Cathedral is located in Katajanokka near the South harbour. The cathedral was designed by Alexander Gornostajev, and built in 1868. It is the largest orthodox church in Western Europe.

The Temppeliaukio Church is built into solid rock with unfinished granite walls. It was designed by Timo and Tuomo Suomalainen and completed in 1969. More than seven hundred persons can be seated under its beautiful cupola made of copper and glass.

The Helsinki railway station was designed by Eliel Saarinen. This impressive granite building which was inaugurated in 1919, is one of the most famous examples of Finnish architecture. The giant granite guards are sculpted by Emil Wikström. Helsinki's main metro station is connected to the railway station (left).

The Glass Palace (Lasipalatsi) in Mannerheimintie represents functionalism. It was completed in 1935 and designed by architects Rewell, Kokko and Riihimäki. The building is now used as a media centre (next spread).

Art in all its forms played an important part in Helsinki´s Cultural Year programme.

"The Crystal" (Kide) a sound and light performance by Kari Leppänen and Peter Ch. Butter is a symbol of the eight Cultural Cities in Europe in the year 2000.

In the forefront, model Maarit Heikkilä in front of the spectacular creation (left).

Kiasma, the Museum of Contemporary Art, is a combined museum, living room and activity centre.

It features Finnish and international contemporary art, multimedia presentations as well as dance performances and cinema. The building was designed by Steven Holl, and completed in 1998 (bottom).

The Finlandia Hall is the number one venue for concerts, congresses and conferences.
The main building was completed in 1971 and the congress wing in 1975. It was designed by Alvar Aalto (1898-1976) (top).

This statue of C.G.E. Mannerheim, Commander-in-Chief of the Finnish army during the Second World War and President of Finland in 1944-46, was sculpted by Aimo Tukiainen in 1960.

The monumental House of Parliament is a massive neo-classical granite building designed by J.S. Sirén. It was built in 1925-31.
Two hundred Members of Parliament are selected every fourth year.

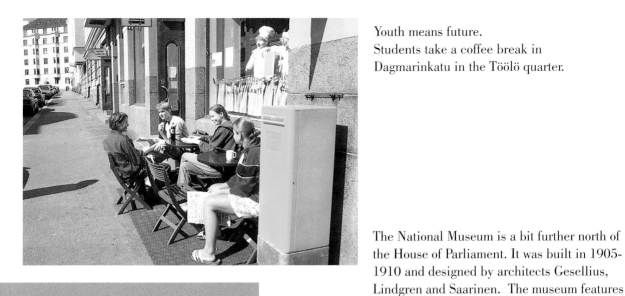

Youth means future.
Students take a coffee break in
Dagmarinkatu in the Töölö quarter.

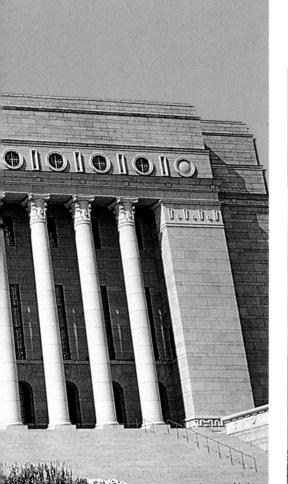

The National Museum is a bit further north of
the House of Parliament. It was built in 1905-
1910 and designed by architects Gesellius,
Lindgren and Saarinen. The museum features
archaeological, historical, numismatic and
ethnological collections which are the result of
170 years of work and research (bottom).

Finland's most popular amusement park, Linnanmäki, is an exciting experience for both young and old, with a breath-taking roller coaster, all kinds of carousels, and a lot of new surprising gadgets and interesting programmes. (left)

The Botanical Garden of Helsinki University is located 10 minutes by foot from the Helsinki railway station. This green oasis, designed by Franz Faldermann of St. Petersburg, was opened to the public in 1833. The picture shows the big greenhouse, which was finished in 1832. (right, top)
The botanical garden contains many exotic plants. One of these is the Paraná giant water-lily (Victoria cruciana) from North Argentina.
Guided tours are arranged for visitors during the whole year.

The Women's Ten Kilometre Run takes place at the end of May each year. It is a joyful event, and many participants dress up in colourful costumes. Every participant gets a prize (bottom).

The Olympic Stadium can seat 40.000 spectators. The track-and-field competition between Finland and Sweden which is arranged every second year is an extremely popular event.

The 72 meters high stadium tower offers a magnificent view over the city (left).

The statue of Paavo Nurmi (1897-1973), the most famous long-distance runner in the world, was sculpted by Wäinö Aaltonen in 1952. Nurmi achieved 25 world records, 9 Olympic gold medals and 3 Olympic silver medals.

The Sibelius monument, a memorial to Finland's most famous composer Jean Sibelius (1865-1957) was sculpted by professor Eila Hiltunen in 1967. The monument features hundreds of steel pipes welded together into a majestic structure and a portrait of the composer sculpted on a nearby rock. It is one of Helsinki's most popular tourist attractions (top).

The Finnish National Opera was inaugurated in 1993. This beautiful building facing the Töölönlahti bay was designed by architects Eero Hyvänmäki, Jukka Karhunen and Risto Parkkinen (bottom).

Minna Tervasmäki and Jukka Aromaa in Ogeninia by John Cranuco, the Finnish National Ballet (right).

In spring, it is nice to take a leisurely walk on the ice outside Seurasaari island.

The Seurasaari open-air museum and park offers beautiful sights and interesting events all year around. The museum features old wooden houses, barns and granaries from all over Finland, dating as far back as the 18th century. In summer, here are all kinds of exhibitions and folk dance performances, and Midsummer is celebrated with a huge bonfire.

Opposite the Opera House, on the other side of Töölö Bay, is the Writers' House, Villa Kivi. This refurbished 19th century building comprises of an office and writers' studios.

Here, the Poets' Club arranges regular meetings where the writers and the public can discuss topics of mutual interest.

The Urho Kekkonen museum in Tamminiemi is the former residence of President Urho Kekkonen (1900-1986). It was opened to the public in 1987. The interior is exactly as it was during Kekkonen's time. A visit to this museum can be combined with a trip to the nearby Seurasaari open-air museum.

Puu-Käpylä is a picturesque neighbourhood with colourful wooden houses and attractive modern buildings. The old part dates back to the 1920s, and is one of the finest examples of the classicism prevailing at that time.

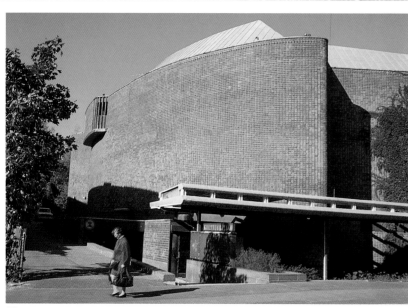

These Art Nouveau-style buildings at Pitkäsilta (The Long Bridge) are from 1906-1912 (left, top).

In the Hakaniemi market square, the commerce is lively as usual. On the northern side of the square is the Hakaniemi market hall and behind it the Arena house built in the 1920s, and designed by Lars Sonck. Helsinki's very first radio programme was transmitted from this house in 1924 (top).

Kaupunginteatteri (The Helsinki City Theatre) has three stages. The beautiful and exceptional building was designed by Timo Penttilä, and completed in 1967 (top),

The Helsinki Hall of Culture is a red-brick building designed by Alvar Aalto. The acoustics in its concert hall is said to be so good that the audience in the back can hear a match falling on the stage floor (left).

A Historical Overview

The Swedish King Gustavus I Vasa founded the town in 1550 on the estuary of the river Vantaa as a competitive partner to Tallinn, which was an important trading port in the Baltic sea area.

For the first couple of centuries life in Helsinki was marked by warfare and tragedies. During the Great Nordic War in 1700-1721, plague and famine killed the majority of its inhabitants, and when the Russian army besieged Helsinki in 1713, a fire destroyed the whole town. It was not until 1748, when Sweden decided to build a stronghold against the growing military threat from Russia, that the number of inhabitants in Helsinki started to increase. During and after the construction of the fortress, a great number of soldiers and craftsmen and their families were transferred to Suomenlinna (or Sveaborg as it was called at the time). Navigation, trade and handicrafts developed rapidly, and the officers and nobility brought new cultural influences and ideas which had a great impact on the country's development.

In the war of 1808-1809, the Russian army invaded Helsinki for the fourth time, and once again the town was largely destroyed by fire. A new city plan was established, and the reconstruction of the town began. In 1809, Finland became a Grand Duchy of the Russian Empire, and Helsinki was named capital in 1812. Czar Alexander I (reigned 1801-1825) wanted to give Helsinki something of the brilliance of the imperial classicism of St. Petersburg, and thus commissioned German architect Carl Ludwig Engel to direct the planning and construction of the city's neo-classical centre. After Finland gained its independence in 1917, the growth of the capital was accelerated.

New city quarters were built, and classicism and functionalism gained ground in Finnish architecture. In the late 1940s and early 1950s Finland still recovered after many years of warfare, but in spite of that, the Olympic Games of 1952 were successfully carried out in Helsinki.

During the period of industrialization and urbanization, Helsinki grew rapidly. New suburbs were built for people who migrated from the rural areas. The 1960s saw the strongest migration movement so far. From the 1970s, Helsinki's role as a European city and host for many big international events has become more accentuated than before. Helsinki was the host city for the first Conference on Security and Co-operation in Europe in 1975. The European Union chairmanship in 1999 strengthened Helsinki's reputation as an ideal host for prestigious international conferences. In the same year, Helsinki was chosen as one of the Cultural Capitals of Europe.

Today, Helsinki is known all over the world as a dynamic city with a rich and diverse culture and outstanding technical know-how and information technology.

The Power Plant Museum is located in the birthplace of Helsinki, near the estuary of the Vantaa river. This old power plant was shut down in the beginning of the 1970s.

Culture and Entertainment

The cultural life in Helsinki is dynamic and versatile. The numerous theatres and the National Opera offer outstanding performances. The Finlandia Hall facing the Töölö Bay is the best known concert hall in the city. In the Tennis Palace (Tennispalatsi) there is an interesting museum with changing collections, and many cinema theatres. The Finns love cinema, so there are many more of them around. The city has 70 museums, of which some of the best known are the National Museum, Kiasma, the Museum of Contemporary Art, Ateneum – The Museum of Finnish Art, the Helsinki City Art Museum, The Zoological Museum and the Museum of Finnish Architecture and Construction.

The city has numerous art galleries, e.g. in Fredrikinkatu and Kalevankatu.

Kaapelitehdas is a former cable factory that has been transformed into a cultural centre containing exhibition halls, artist studios, art schools, a café and a restaurant.

The Linnanmäki amusement park in Helsinki and the Serena Water Park in the nearby city of Espoo offers entertainment and unforgettable experiences to young as well as older visitors. For the bookworms there are many book stores, the best known being Akateeminen Kirjakauppa (The Academic Bookstore) and Suomalainen Kirjakauppa (The Finnish Bookstore). Helsinki also has a writers' house called – Villa Kivi.

The Helsinki Fair Centre and the Wanha Satama Exhibition Hall arrange numerous informative and entertaining fairs and exhibitions. Helsinki's many nightclubs and restaurants offer delicious food and drinks, music, dancing and entertainment until the wee hours of the morning.

Dancing at a typically Finnish open-air dance floor is called "lava-tanssit" in Finnish. This is an exotic experience worth trying. In Vantaa on the outskirts of Helsinki this can be done at the Pavi dance floor.

The new millennium was celebrated with sparkling fireworks, lilluminatine the nocturnal sky above Eläintarhanlahti bay (top).

Helsinki's 450th anniversary on 12.6. 2000 was celebrated with pomp and splendour.
A spectacular historical parade marched through the city to the accompaniment of drums (right).

Hotels and tourism

Helsinki has about 50 hotels of which about 20 are rated first class. All the hotels are of high standing, offering excellent accommodation and services. There are also about ten comfortable and well equipped hostels. Most of the hotels have a Finnish sauna. For reservations you can contact the Helsinki Expert Hotel Center, e-mail address: *hotel@helsinkiexpert.fi*.

Helsinki is a safe place to visit, with good medical and health services and a low crime rate.
Regular guided sightseeing tours by bus take about an hour, and a tour by the Helsinki tram marked 3T about half an hour. Sightseeing tour boats leave from the Market Square every hour. Day cruises can be booked at the Helsinki Expert Center (see above).
Public transportation services are excellent. Regional tickets are available for 1, 3 or 5 days. Taxis are on call day and night. Domestic and international connections by train, boat and airplane from Helsinki are extremely good.

In summer, tourists are guided by friendly guides in green shirts. We call them "Helsinki-helps".
A guided, so called "cultural walk" is a good way of getting both exercise and knowledge about the architecture and history of Helsinki. Those who do not like walking can use roller skates or bicycles, or take the bus, metro or a tram.

Some of Helsinki's many excellent hotels are Hotel Kämp in Pohjoisesplanadi (bottom), Palace Hotel in Eteläranta , Hotel Torni in Kalevankatu (top), Ramada President Hotel in Rautatiekatu, the Scandic Hotel Intercontinental and Radisson SAS-hotels in Runeberginkatu and Mannerheimintie, as well as Hotel Kalastajatorppa in Munkkiniemi.

Vantaa

The city of Vantaa lies in the northern part of the Helsinki area, about 15 kilometres from the city centre.

Vantaa is a young and dynamic city with thriving industries and outstanding educational institutions. The city's two polytechnics and the complementary education centre of the Helsinki University have contacts to many international institutions in their respective fields. This enables them to create fruitful connections and educate outstanding professionals.

The Helsinki-Vantaa airport (bottom) is Finland's gateway to the world. The airport is used by over one hundred charter-flight companies, and it has been officially rated as one of the best airports in the world. The Finnish airline company Finnair maintains regular flights to about 40 destinations all over the world and to 20 destinations in Finland.

A visit to the Finnish Science Centre Heureka in Vantaa is a thrilling experience. Its permanent and temporary exhibitions are both fantastic and intriguing, and its Verne-theatre offers a variety of programmes on all kinds of topical scientific subjects. For children, there are lots of interesting things to see and do. (top)

Pyhän Laurin kirkko (the St. Lawrence church), built in 1494, is one of the best known tourist attractions in Vantaa. It is also a popular wedding church. (right)

Espoo

The city of Espoo is part of the Greater Helsinki area. It is the second biggest city in Finland. The population of Espoo has a high level of education. Many of them are multi-lingual and internationally orientated, which is a prerequisite for the local industries to operate successfully on the international arena.

The Tapiola region in Espoo is the biggest know-how centre in Northern Europe. The Helsinki University of Technology (bottom) and the Technical Research Centre of Finland are located here. Besides offering education and research they have connections to a variety of institutions and industries all over the world.

The museum and former studio-home of famous Finnish painter Akseli Gallén-Kallela (1865-1931) is located in Tarvaspää in the City of Espoo. The museum is a very popular tourist attraction. It also has a café, serving typically Finnish rolls and pastries. (top)

The Espoo Cultural Centre in Tapiola is an important venue for all kinds of cultural activities, such as art exhibitions, concerts and congresses. It also comprises a library. The modern building was designed by A. Sipinen, and completed in 1989. (left)

The headquarters of the Nokia corporation is located in Keilalahti, Espoo. (bottom)

The National Park of Nuuksio lies about 30 kilometres from Helsinki. The major part of this beautiful park, which is one of Europe's last wilderness areas, is situated in the city of Espoo.
The park offers all kinds of leisure activities, such as horse-riding, which has been practiced here for a long time.

The Greater Helsinki Area consists of 12 independent municipalities. The whole area has 1,7 million inhabitants, and the average educational level is the highest in the country. The trade, service and IT-sectors are their main sources of income. Today, Helsinki is one of Europe's most prominent cities in the IT-field.

Among the best known sights in this area is the home of composer Jean Sibelius in Järvenpää, the studio of painter Pekka Halonen in Tuusula, the studio-museum of painter Akseli Gallén-Kallela in Tarvaspää in the city of Espoo, and the studio/home of architects Gesellius, Lindgren and Saarinen in Hvitträsk, Kirkkonummi. The National Park of Nuuksio is a beautiful protected wilderness area of approximately 17 square kilometres stretching over Espoo, Vihti and Kirkkonummi.

One of the best known painters' studios in Finland is Halosenniemi, the house of Pekka Halonen (1865-1933) in Tuusula , designed by the painter himself (top).

The studio and living quarters of the great architects Gesellius, Lindgren and Saarinen, situated in the town of Kirkkonummi near lake Hvitträsk, was built in 1904. The three architects designed the buildings in the National-Romantic and Art Nouveau styles. The houses, decorated with exquisite taste and attention to detail, can be visited. There is also a very good restaurant.

In the municipalities around Helsinki there are lots of interesting sights and services. At the Rehndahl animal farm in Kirkkonummi, there are all kinds of domestic animals.
Facilities for conferences, parties and sauna are also available. The hostess Susanne Hildén is very fond of her horses. (left)